Note to parents

This book contains a wealth of beautiful illustrations showing familiar objects that young children will enjoy identifying.

You will also find numerous opportunities to introduce concepts such as color, shape, and number. You can help to reinforce your child's early learning skills by playing some of the games suggested on pages 36-37.

Talking about pictures is an excellent way to help your child develop verbal fluency and a rich vocabulary. By drawing attention to favorite words, you can introduce the idea of printed language. Encourage your child to look at the details in the pictures. This visual skill will be important later for learning to read.

Remember—always go at your child's pace and give constant praise. Your help and encouragement will enable your child to make the most of the learning experiences this book has to offer.

KINGFISHER
Larousse Kingfisher Chambers Inc.
95 Madison Avenue
New York, New York 10016

First published by Kingfisher 1996
2 4 6 8 10 9 7 5 3

This edition produced for Baby's First Book Club®
Bristol, PA 19907

LIBRARY OF CONGRESS CATALOGING-IN-PUBLICATION DATA
Baker, Alan.
Little Rabbits' first word book / Alan Baker—1st ed.
p.   cm.
Summary: Rabbits present words and matching pictures grouped under
such topics as toys, food, things that move, animals, and drawing
and painting. Includes simple word and concept games.
1. Vocabulary—juvenile literature   [1. Vocabulary]   I. Title.
PE1449.B29   1996
428.1—dc20   96-7359 CIP AC

ISBN 1-881445-89-5

Additional text by Kate Hayden
Designed by Caroline Johnson

Printed in Singapore

Little Rabbits'
First Word Book

Alan Baker

Baby's First Book Club®

Clothes

shoes

cap

socks

buttons

jacket

shirt

underpants

sweater

dress

pants

vest

rain
boots

7

In the kitchen

cup

saucer

plate

teapot

mug

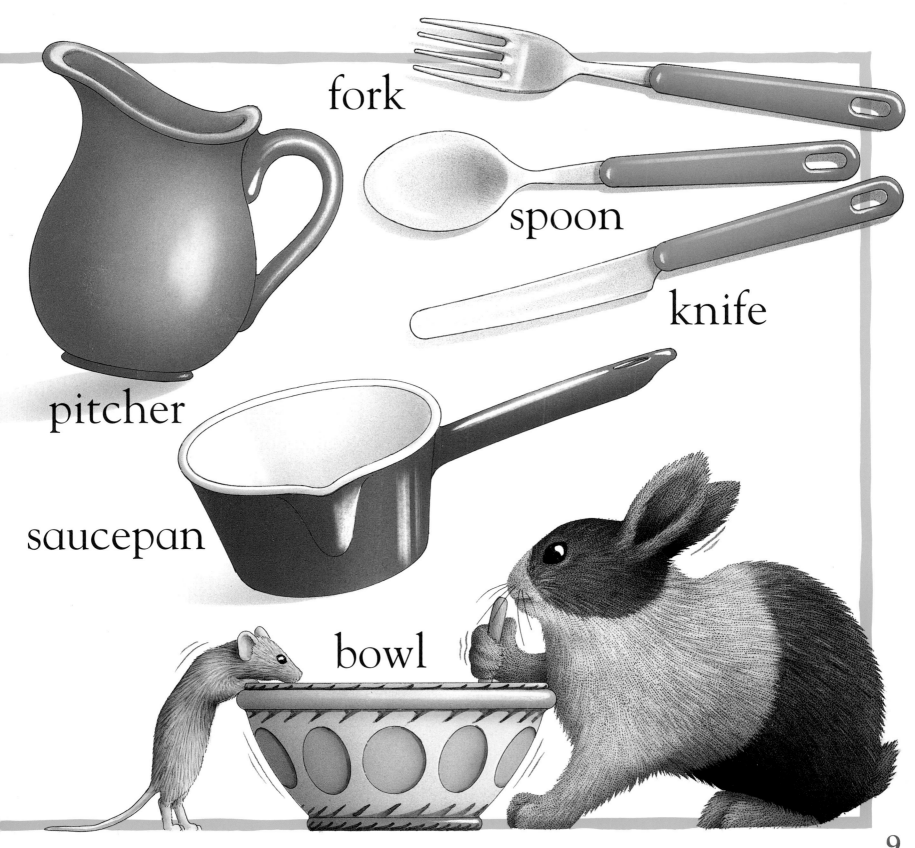

fork

spoon

knife

pitcher

saucepan

bowl

9

Toys

telephone

doll

wagon

blocks

rattle

puzzle

beads

cards

train

11

Animals

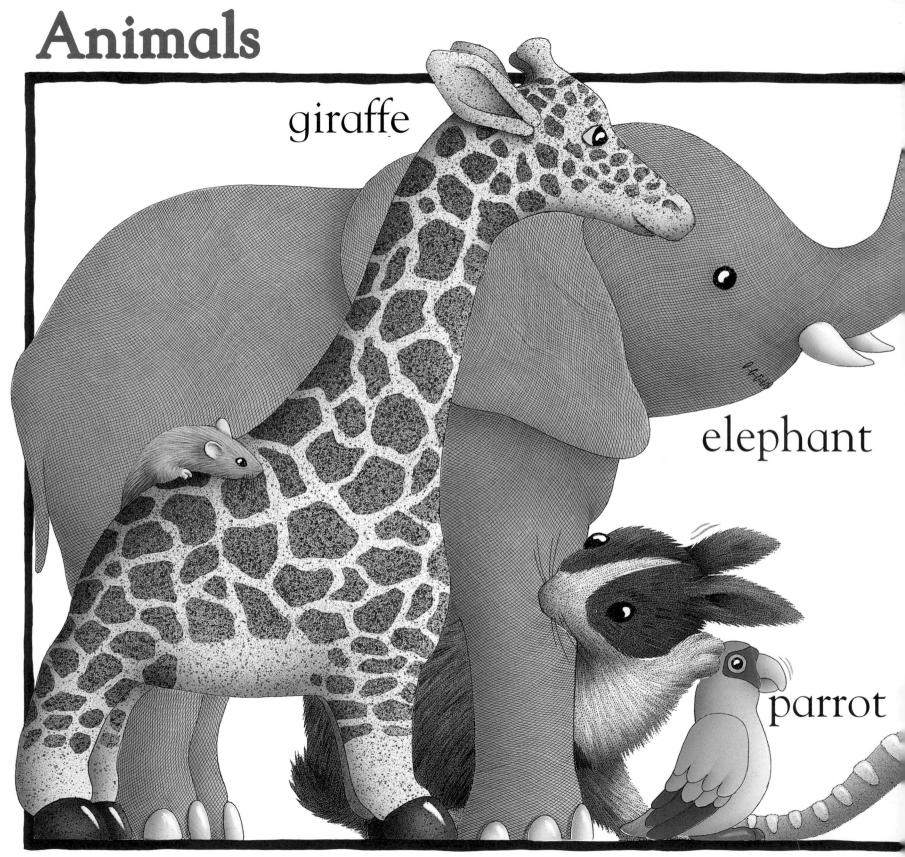

giraffe

elephant

parrot

tiger

monkey

crocodile

kangaroo

lion

panda

zebra

snake

13

Around the house

cushion

books

keys

dustpan

brush

broom

picture

chair

lamp

vase

table

15

In the garden

shovel

worm

ant

seeds

wheelbarrow

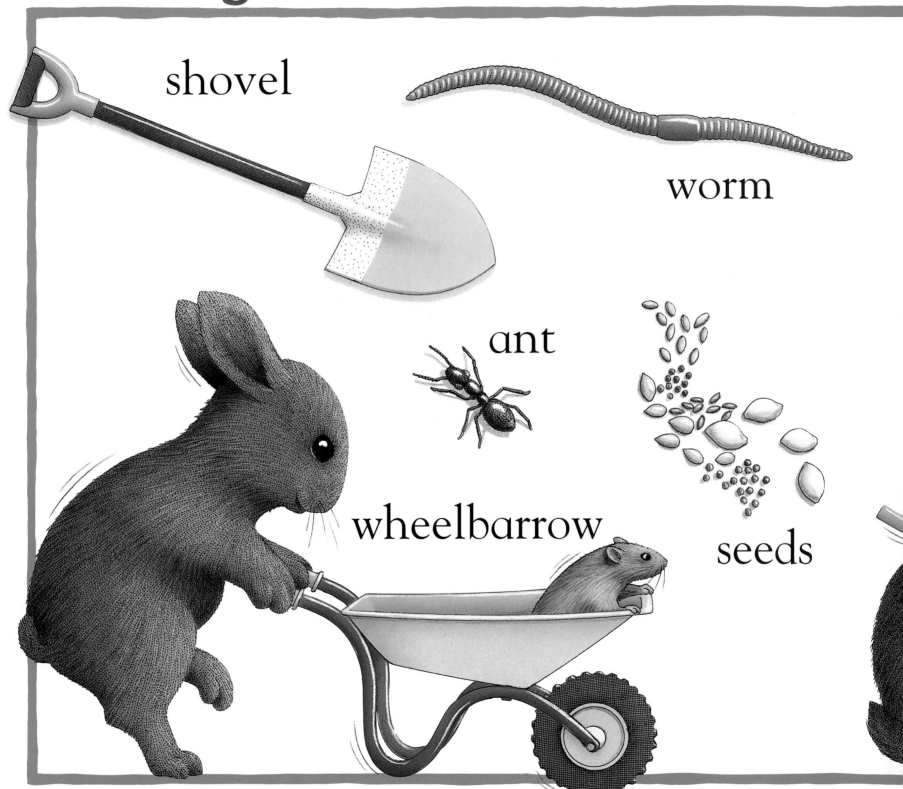

flower

flowerpot

leaf

watering can

rake

Making a noise

whistle

recorder

drum

flute

tambourine

maracas

xylophone

trumpet

bell

Drawing and painting

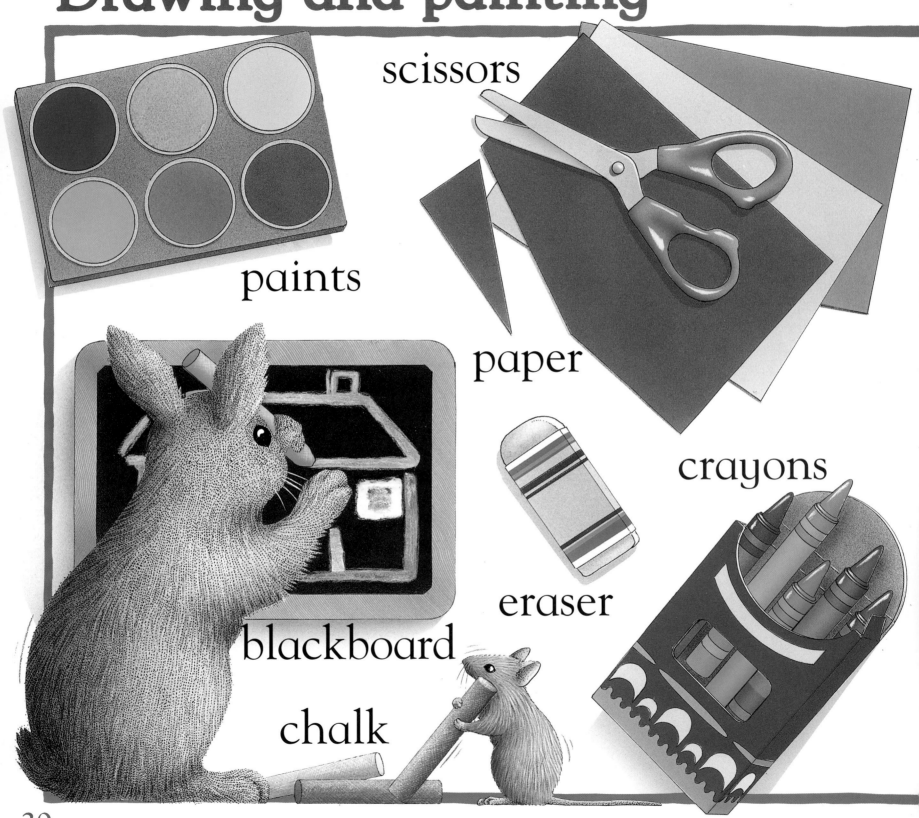

scissors

paints

paper

crayons

eraser

blackboard

chalk

ruler

felt-tip pens

paintbrushes

pencil

easel

21

Colors

yellow

blue

red

black

lemon

strawberries

beetle

butterfly

pumpkin

purple

brown

green

orange

rabbit

frog

grapes

23

Shapes

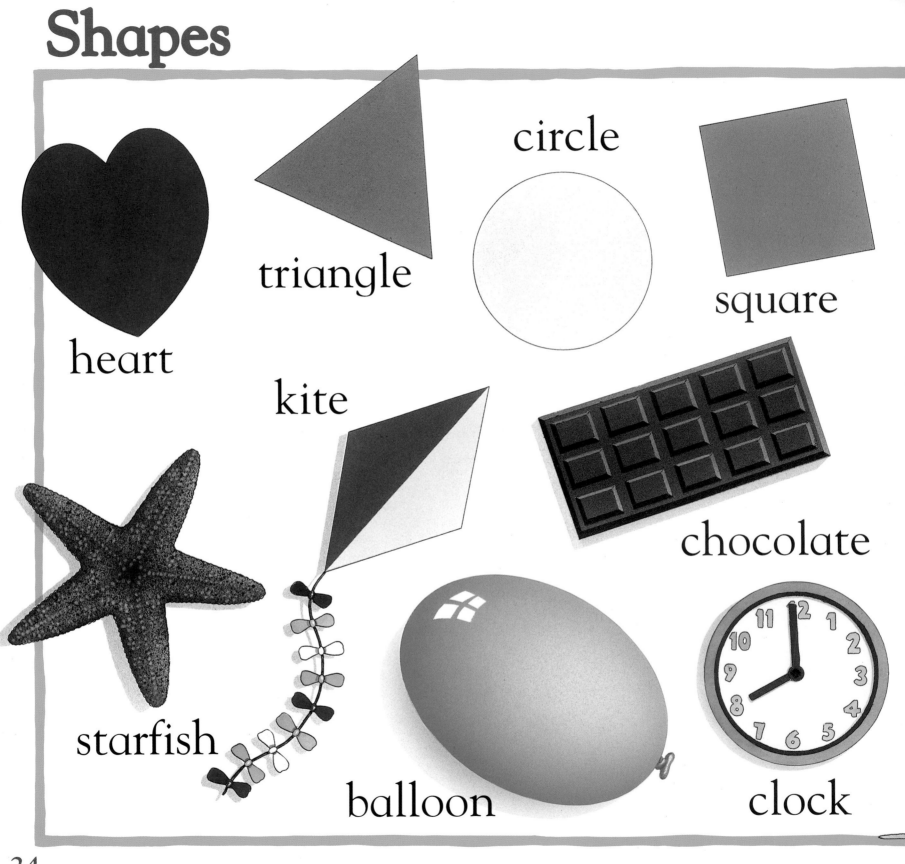

heart

triangle

circle

square

kite

chocolate

starfish

balloon

clock

diamond

star

oval

rectangle

valentine

washcloth

flags

25

At the park

swing

umbrella

bench

bicycle

tree

slide

seesaw

27

Things to eat

cookies

sandwich

apple

banana

carrots

cheese

orange

noodles

corn

tomato

yogurt

lettuce

ice cream

On the farm

pig

chicks

horse

cow

goat

rooster

dog

duck

hen

sheep

tractor

31

Bathtime

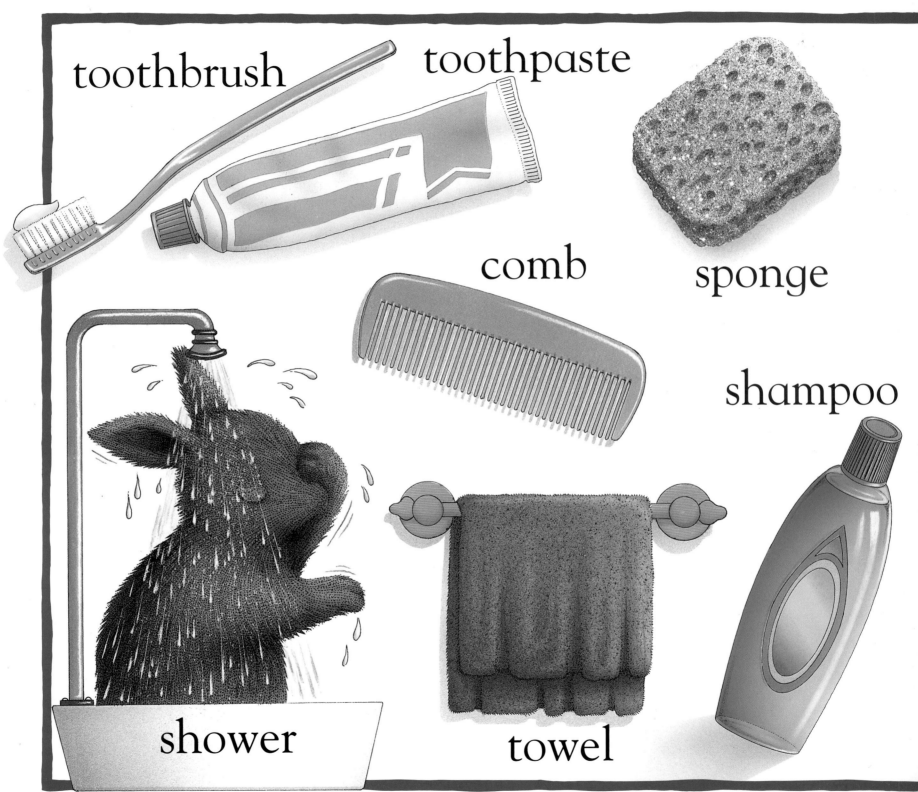

toothbrush

toothpaste

sponge

comb

shampoo

shower

towel

hairbrush

bubbles

soap

talcum powder

mirror

bathtub

33

Bedtime

quilt

slippers

bathrobe

blanket

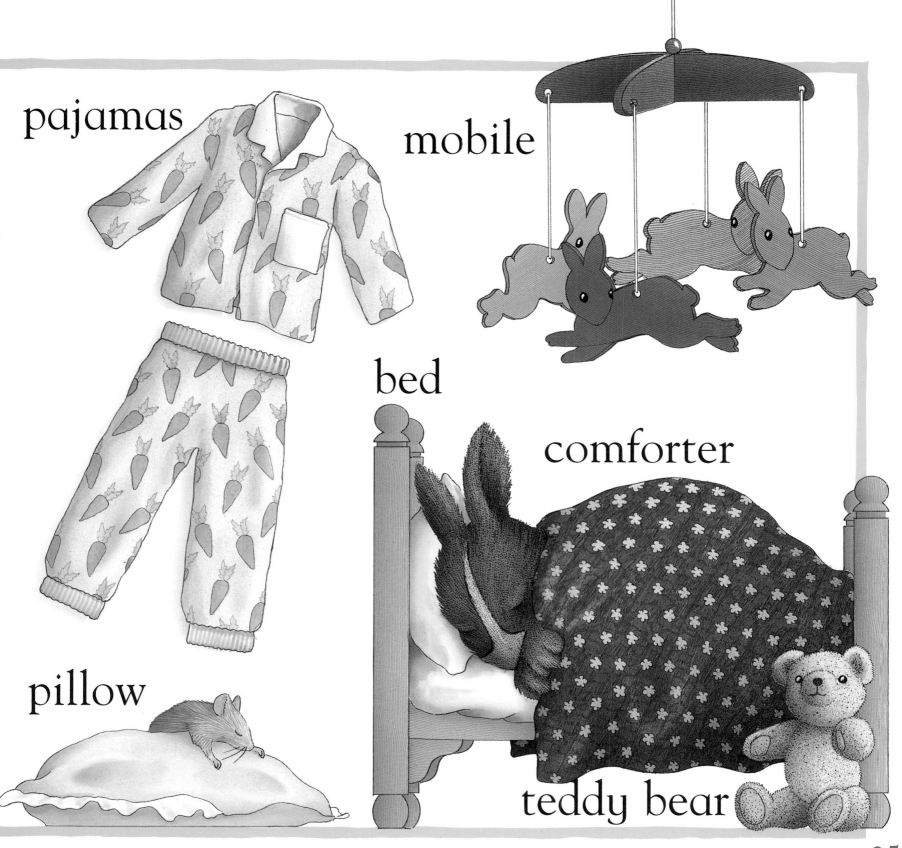

pajamas

mobile

bed

comforter

pillow

teddy bear

35

Games to play

Playing these games with your child makes learning to recognize colors and shapes more fun. They will help develop observation as well as verbal, sorting, and matching skills.

Where's the mouse?
Ask your child to look for the little brown mouse that appears in every scene. Help him or her to describe what the mouse is doing.

Who says moo? (pages 30-31)
Very young children love identifying and imitating animal noises. See if your child can find the animal to match the noises you make. Alternatively, point to an animal and ask your child to make the right noise.

Color match (pages 22-23)
Ask your child to say what is blue on these pages. Continue through the other six colors, matching each brushstroke to the fruit or animal of the same color.

Shape match (pages 24-25)
Help your child to find an object to match each of the two-dimensional shapes shown at the top of these pages. Introduce the names of some of the shapes.

What is round?
Help your child to look for round shapes or circles on some pages. Examples are: buttons (page 6), plate (page 8), beads, train wheels (pages 10-11), tambourine (page 18), paint box colors (page 20), circle and clock (page 24), wheels (page 26), bubbles (page 33).

Big and little (pages 12-13)
Ask your child which is the biggest animal and which is the smallest in this scene. Extend the discussion to other characteristics, for example: Who can fly? Who has stripes? Who can jump?

Match the words and pictures.

ant
ball
cushion
drum
fork
hairbrush
kite
leaf
orange
paints
pitcher
shoes
telephone
worm
yogurt

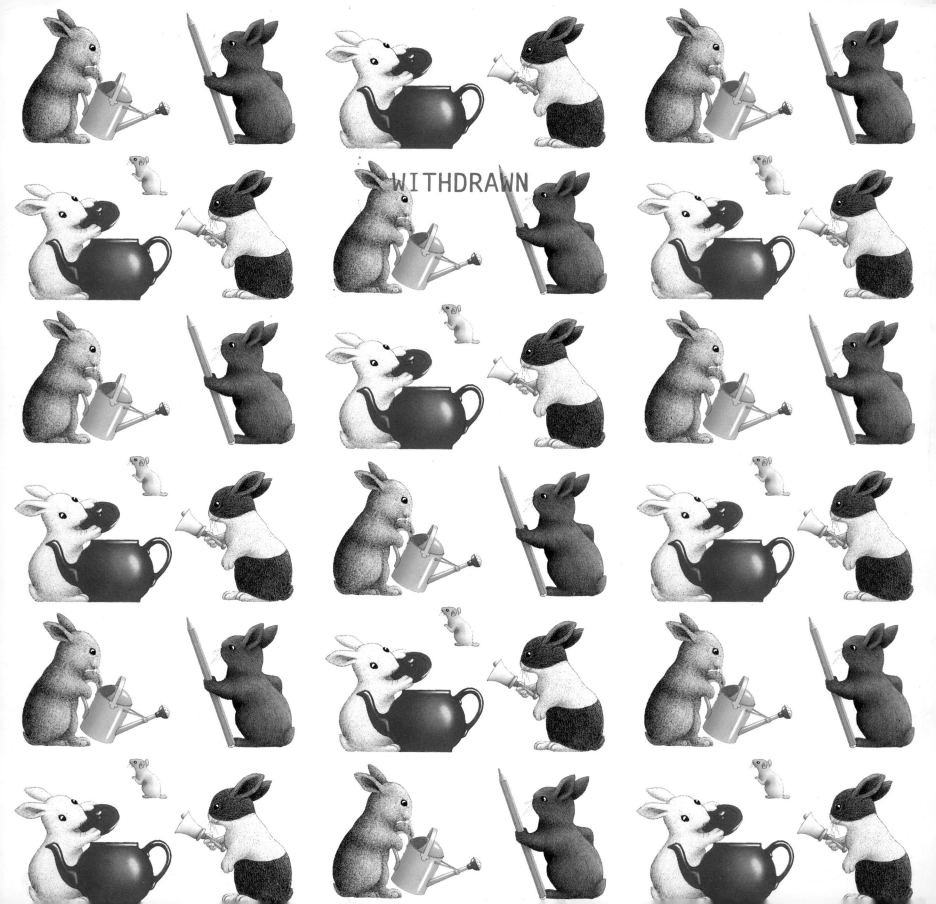